Burnt Pages, Rewritten Stories

A Journey of Grieving, Healing & Becoming

Shyama Kotecha

India | USA | UK

Made with ❤ on the BookLeaf Publishing Platform
www.bookleafpub.in
www.bookleafpub.com

Dedication

For those navigating life's many chapters — the
uncertain, the exciting, the quiet in-between.

For those balancing love and loss, dreams and chaos,
growth and stillness, all at once.

For the ones still unfolding, learning to move slowly,
gently, fiercely and moreover - *honestly and
unapologetically.*

This book is for you — for your strength, your heart and
your journey.

May these words be a *tight hug and gentle anchor,*
grounding you as you navigate **your own becoming.**

Preface

This book began as a quiet return to writing, to feeling, to myself.

Over the last couple of years, I found myself sitting with a lot of emotions I didn't always know how to name. So, I wrote. Not to find answers but just to make space. These poems reflect moments of confusion, uncertainty, heartbreak, grief, hope, self-acceptance, rebuilding confidence and everything in between.

The journey of this book starts with confusion and heartbreak — the kind that leaves you sitting in silence. It then moves through the many layers of growing up: equations that shift, career crossroads, losing your sense of self — and then slowly, scarily, gently, finding it again. Towards the end, the poems turn softer, more hopeful — *a quiet reminder that even after all the despair and dark, there's still light.*

There's no single story here. Just honest words from different days, different versions of me.

This book is for anyone trying to hold space for everything at once — love and doubt, dreams and decisions, pressure and pause. *It's for the ones who are still learning to be okay with who and where they are.*

In the beginning, you may find echoes of your own heartbreak—grief, confusion, the quiet ache of feeling lost.
But as you turn the pages, I hope my words begin to rise beside you—growing steadier, stronger—until they stand with you like light after a long night, gently guiding you forward, wherever you are in your journey.

Let this book be a gentle reminder: you are not lost, just becoming.

Acknowledgements

To everyone who has ever held space for me — in silence,
in conversation, in presence, in prayers — *thank you.*

To the heartbreaks, the pauses, the sleepless nights and the
setbacks that shaped these pages — *you were all
necessary.*

To my family and friends, for your quiet love, loud
encouragement and unwavering belief in me, even when I
didn't see it myself — *I'm deeply grateful.*

And to every reader holding this book in their hands —
thank you for making space in your life for my words.
*I hope they meet you where you are and walk with you a
while.*

1. I Walked Into the Fire

Loving you felt like a flame
I walked into alone.
I knew it wasn't safe in there,
But still—I called it home.

I saw the smoke, I smelled the burn,
But couldn't turn away.
You were inside, and part of me
Just needed you to stay.

I didn't hope to save it all,
Just something small and true—
Some piece of us not touched by fire,
Some proof I once had you.

You were the fire—I was the brave,
The fool who ran, the one who gave.
And if I burned, at least I'll know—
I didn't leave love's ghost to grow.

It hurt. It broke. It took my breath.
I lost more than I knew.
But worse than burning in that house
Was walking past you.

I gave my love, I gave my fight,
I stayed when it got hard.
And now the house is gone, but still—
I keep that kind of heart.

No, I'm not proud of every scar,
But I'm proud I didn't run.
There's peace in knowing what I gave,
Even when we're done.

You were the fire. I was the spark
That tried to light the dark.
And though I couldn't pull you out,
I never missed the mark.

2. Despite the Dark

It's easy to love what shines so bright,
The golden, gleaming part—
But harder still to hold the night
That lives inside a heart.

I didn't love you *just because*
You smiled or played the role—
I loved you through the quiet flaws
That never made you whole.

They say love blooms *because of* light,
But ours was something more—
I loved you *despite of* every storm
That shook you to your core.

I saw the storm behind your eyes,
The weight you tried to hide—
And still I stayed, through every shade
That chased the light inside.

Not every day was soft or kind,
Not every word was sweet—
But loving you *despite* the cracks
Was love that felt complete.

I didn't choose you for the sun,
Or wait for skies to clear—
I lit a candle in your dark
And held it near and dear.

Because love, real love, is not a prize
For who we are on stage—
It's written in the shadowed lines
We carry page by page.

So don't ask me why I stayed so long,
Or why I didn't flee—
Loving you despite it all
Was loving truthfully.

3. Promises, Unmatched

You were the *"promises are meant to break"* kind,
I was the *"pinky swear and seal it"* mind.
You loved with loopholes, with ways to bend,
I held on like forever was the end.

You called it "real," I called it fear,
You vanished when I drew you near.
I built a home in every word you said,
While you kept doors half-closed instead.

I trusted in the vows we made,
Believed in words that slowly fade.
I saw the future in your eyes,
But you, you left me with goodbyes.

You laughed at vows, I held them tight—
You chased the thrill, I chose the right.
I gave all of me, a heart unsealed,
While you kept parts of yours concealed.

I held my breath when you'd say, *"I swear,"*
I waited for actions to match the air.
But you were the storm I couldn't fight,
The fleeting love that left no light.

You said that promises weren't meant to last,
That I should've known better, left the past.
But how could I have learned to let it go,
When all I knew was love and trust in tow?

Maybe love is not about the length,
Or how much you're willing to extend your strength.
Maybe it's about the courage to stand,
And walk away when you don't understand.

So next time, I'll love, but with both eyes wide,
No more pinky promises to those who hide.
I'll build my own walls and hold them strong,
No more waiting for a love that's wrong.

You were the echo, I was the sound—
But I won't beg to be kept around.
The next promise I make will be to me,
To never settle for the love I couldn't see.

4. It's beautiful, isn't it?

The moon is beautiful, isn't it?
We sat together, hearts aligned,
Fingers tracing lines that didn't fit,
But for a moment, we didn't mind.

In silence, we spoke with our eyes,
The world outside could disappear—
You told me you'd love me through all the lies,
I believed it, and held you near.

But love isn't just whispered promises,
It's more than holding hands in the dark.
And slowly, what once felt endless,
Started to crumble, leaving no spark.

I felt you drift in little ways,
Not with anger, but quiet withdrawal—
You didn't fight, you didn't stay,
And I couldn't make you feel it all.

We still tried, held on for what?
For something that was never meant to last—
Afraid to speak the truth, too scared to stop,
We kept running, ignoring the past.

Now, here we are, just side by side,
The silence heavier than the weight of words—
You look at me, I look at you, but we can't hide,
The love that was - has gone, without a word.

We've had our time, we've had our place—
But love, like the day, fades into it,
And we both know it's time to let go, to embrace
The sunset is beautiful, isn't it?

5. The Gift of Perspective

Thank you for the best gift—
Perspective, in your wake.
Before you, I feared the loss,
The heartache love could break.

I held my heart with trembling hands,
Afraid to let it fall—
The thought of losing someone close
Was my greatest fear of all.

But after you, I see it clear—
The fear was never true.
It wasn't love I should have feared,
But losing what's inside of you.

Now I fear the life I'd settle for,
The one that drains my soul—
Where I chase what isn't mine,
And lose myself to feel whole.

I spent so long fearing I'd lose you,
I didn't see I'd lost my way—
In trying to keep a piece of you,
I let myself slip away.

I gave so much, I gave it all,
Till nothing much remained—
I looked for love outside of me
And forgot where I'd been changed.

I'd rather walk alone in truth
Than stay in shadows, blind—
For love that asks you to let go
Of everything you are, is not kind.

I won't lose myself again,
I won't chase a lie—
For the greatest loss of all
Is giving up what makes you fly.

6. The Desire to Disappear

Every time I've felt the need to fade,
To vanish, to slip into shadows, afraid—
I tell myself I want to be alone,
To leave it all, to just be unknown.

I crave the silence, the absence of sound,
To disappear where no eyes are found.
The weight of the world feels too much to bear,
So I wish to be lost, just out of despair.

But deep in the quiet, I hear a plea,
A whisper inside that won't let me be.
It says, *"You want to be lost, but found too,
Because even in darkness, you crave something true."*

I want to hide, to drift far away,
But there's something inside that makes me stay.
I seek the comfort of being unseen,
Yet I wish to be found in places unseen.

I want to vanish, but not from the world—
I want to disappear, then have someone unfurl
The parts of me that I try to disguise,
To be found again, beneath the lies.

So every time I think I want to escape,
To slip through the cracks and change my shape,
I realize I don't want to disappear alone—
I just need someone to bring me back home.

7. In the Quiet Moments

The more I grow, the more I've learned,
That love isn't just the fires that burn.
It's not the fireworks that light the night,
But the flickers, the steady warmth, the quiet light.

There was a time I craved the grand,
The sweeping gestures, the outstretched hand.
A candlelit dinner, a lavish surprise,
A love that dazzles with bright, wide eyes.

But now, with age, I see it clear—
Love's found in moments, in what's near.
It's not in the rush, not in the show,
But in the gentle ways we let each other grow.

A cup of tea on a quiet morning,
The soft *"How was your day?"* without warning.
A text to say you're thinking of me,
Without needing a reason, without needing a plea.

Every now and then, yes, a grand gesture's nice,
A grand romantic sweep, a love so precise.
But it's in the waiting, the in-between,
That love grows strong, steady and unseen.

It's in the little things that keep us whole,
The random touches, the heart to soul.
It's not about the once-in-a-lifetime surprise,
But the everyday care that never dies.

Like the way you listen when I need to speak,
Or hold me close when I'm feeling weak.
It's the laughter we share over a simple meal,
The comfort in silence, the way you make me feel.

It's the slow, consistent rhythm that tells the tale,
The warmth that's steady, that never goes stale.
The way we know each other's needs without words,
The soft gestures, the kindest of thirds.

The more I grow, the more I realize,
That love's not in the grand or the prize.
It's in the quiet moments, the simple ways,
The small efforts that carry us through the days.

Because the grand gestures may come and go,
But it's the small efforts that truly show—

That you're loved, that you're cared for, that you matter,
Not in the big acts but in the moments that scatter.

8. What is Love?

Love isn't just a feeling, it's a choice,
A decision we make, a steady voice.
It's choosing to stay when the road gets tough,
And deciding together, even when enough's enough.

Love is a responsibility, strong and true,
A promise to carry, no matter what we go through.
It's showing up when we don't feel our best,
And lifting each other when life puts us to the test.

Love is a decision, clear and pure,
A commitment we make, of that I'm sure.
It's the daily act of choosing to be near,
And making space for the one we hold dear.

Love is a prayer, whispered with care,
In the quiet of night, or moments we share.
It's trusting in what we can't always see,
And hoping for the best, for you and me.

Love is a friendship, built on trust,
A foundation we nurture, steady and just.
It's laughter in silence, joy in the small,
A bond that grows stronger, through it all.

Love is consideration, gentle and kind,
Thinking of you first, in body and mind.
It's noticing the little things, the quiet ways,
That show we care, beyond words or praise.

Love is becoming the best you can be,
Not perfect—but better, for them and for me.
It's growth with intention, a silent vow,
To heal what hurts and show up now.

Love is showing up, come storm or shine,
When nothing feels certain, but you still align.
It's presence in moments both bitter and sweet,
It's staying grounded when life hits repeat.

Love is refusing to walk away,
Even when words get lost, and skies turn grey.
It's fighting for "us" through every rough patch,
Knowing what's real is worth the scratch.

And when all the noise has faded to dust,
What remains is the bond, the quiet trust.

It's not always magic, or fireworks above—
But this, right here, is the *truth of love.*

9. Giving Up vs Letting Go

Giving up feels like a heavy stone,
A choice to quit when you're left alone.
It's the weight of defeat, the silence loud,
The shattering dream beneath a dark cloud.

It's the surrender to doubt, the end of the fight,
The burning out of a fading light.
You stop because it's easier to run,
To pretend that the battle's already won.

But letting go—*oh*, that's different, you see,
It's not surrender, it's setting yourself free.
It's releasing what never truly fit,
And walking away from the things that quit.

Letting go isn't about giving in,
It's the strength to accept what you cannot win.
It's realizing that not all things are meant to stay,
And having the courage to let them fade away.

Giving up is a wound that keeps bleeding,
While letting go is a healing, freeing feeling.
It's knowing your worth, your dreams, your path—
And no longer chasing what makes you crash.

So don't confuse the two, don't mistake the art,
Giving up is the end, letting go is the start.
One holds you back, while the other lets you soar—
Let go of what doesn't serve you anymore.

10. Romanticizing the Journey

You romanticize the journey to rationalize the pain,
Turning each tear into a tale,
As if the ache could somehow heal
If wrapped in words we fail.

I see the beauty in the broken,
The strength inside the fall—
I don't need to make it shine
To know how much I've burned at all.

We say the loss was part of fate,
That brokenness was meant—
But deep inside, we know it's just
A way to numb the scent.

The pain doesn't need a meaning,
It doesn't need a rhyme—
Sometimes it's just the weight we bear
Through quiet, empty time.

You turn each scar into a crown,
And wear it like a story told—
But I've learned to carry what I've lost,
To walk without regret, so bold.

We romanticize the journey,
To make the hurt feel right—
But sometimes, it's just too much to carry
In the stillness of the night.

And in the end, I don't need to shine
What's already there inside—
I'll carry it and let it be,
Without the need to hide.

11. The Maze Within

There's a storm inside, a quiet war,
A battle I fight behind every door.
Anxiety whispers its ruthless refrain,
Doubt in my heart like a shadow remains.

The mirror's gaze feels sharp, unkind,
A fractured reflection I cannot unbind.
Too much, not enough—what's the measure of worth,
When the world holds a scale for your body since birth?

Career paths stretch like a forking road,
Each step unsure, with a heavier load.
What's the right choice? Where should I stand?
Dreams slip away like grains of sand.

Friendships unravel, threads pulled apart,
Once woven with love, now strained in the heart.
The silence between us, a canyon too wide,
I wonder where we lost the light inside.

Relationships falter, the cracks run deep,
Words left unsaid, and promises we keep.
A puzzle unsolved, love's tangled art,
How do I heal what tears at my heart?

Every corner I turn, a question awaits,
Each answer elusive, wrapped in my fates.
I long for escape, a path that is clear,
But the maze only echoes my growing fear.

Yet somewhere within, a voice still small,
It whispers of strength to rise from the fall.
In the midst of the chaos, I'll learn to breathe,
To shed the old burdens and begin to believe.

Perhaps in this maze, I'm not meant to flee,
But to find the courage to simply be me.
For though the way out feels distant, unsure,
I'll build it myself—step by step, I'll endure.

12. The Weight of Twenty

I am twenty-something, caught in the haze,
A labyrinth of lost and endless days.
Friends once close now drift like the tide,
Their laughter echoes, yet none abide.

Dreams, bold and bright, once kissed my brow,
But they slip through my fingers—where are they now?
The race to "ahead" is a race undefined,
Yet I'm tethered to whispers of a child left behind.

The mirror shows me a face I don't know,
A patchwork of questions that refuse to grow.
Who am I meant to be? What path to chart?
These riddles carve valleys deep in my heart.

The clock is a phantom, swift and unkind,
It steals my moments and clouds my mind.
Yesterday's laughter feels a breath away,
But here I stand, in the harsh light of today.

I long for the ease of swings and sun,
When worries dissolved with the day undone.
But adulthood knocks with its iron-clad fist,
A life to build, a checklist to tick.

Still, within me, a flicker remains,
A child who believes in breaking chains.
So I hold on to dreams, though tattered they be,
And hope time's puzzle grants clarity.

For in this storm of struggle and strife,
Perhaps I'm just learning the rhythm of life.

13. Roots or Wings?

I'm standing on the edge of all I've known,
A place where memories and roots have grown.
Leaving behind the streets I walked in the rain,
The faces that know my joy, my pain.

The walls of my home still echo my name,
A place of comfort, where no one's to blame.
But I'm walking away, with a heart full of doubt,
Chasing a dream I can't live without.

I feel the weight of the goodbye in my chest,
Leaving the ones who've loved me best.
Mom's soft hands, Dad's subtle care —
I know they'll be waiting but life isn't fair.

Friends who've been there through thick and thin,
Now I'm walking alone, unsure of where to begin.
The laughter we shared, the secrets we kept,
Will fade like the promises I've never wept.

And my younger brother, too young to know,
Why I must leave, why I can't show
Up for his games or hear his day —
I hope he forgives me for walking away.

But the guilt gnaws deep, in the silence of night,
I'm torn between dreams and love's tight grip, so tight.
Will they be okay? Will they be fine?
While I chase a life that isn't mine?

The fear of the unknown, the fear of new things,
The thought of the future, the joy it brings.
But still, I hesitate, as the world calls my name,
I'm scared of the change, of leaving the same.

Will I forget them? Will they forget me?
As I try to be all I can be.
The road ahead is paved with doubt,
But it's time to take the step, to leave and break out.

I'll carry their love, their voices in my ear,
As I face the unknown, my heart full of fear.
The guilt is there, but I know it's true,
To make my mark, I must start anew.

So I'll take the first step, even though it's hard,
Leaving behind what's safe in my backyard.

And though the road is long and steep,
I'll rise and conquer, though the past I keep.

14. The Ones Who've Moved Ahead

They're boarding flights, they're chasing light,
Living their dreams that took off just right.
They laugh in cafés I've never known,
While I sit here, tired and alone.

They post of wins, of doors flung wide,
While I hold failure close and hide.
Their world spins fast in vibrant hues,
Mine's pages marked with missed-out news.

Each morning starts with heavy eyes,
And coffee cold and practiced lies.
I tell myself - *just one more day,*
While joy feels several towns away.

They talk of work and monthly pay,
Of moving in, of moving away.
I talk to walls and whisper plans,
That slip like water through my hands.

I miss the me who used to dream,
Before success became extreme—
Before the charts, the marks, the race,
Before I feared I'd lose my place.

They call it discipline, strength and grind,
But never see what's left behind.
The cracked self-worth, the silent cries,
The shame that hides behind "*I'm fine.*"

And still I try, though knees feel weak,
Though hope plays hide and seek each week.
They left the station long ago,
And I'm still learning how to go.

But maybe time's not running out—
Just taking the scenic route, no doubt.
And though I ache to catch the train,
I'll walk this track through sun and rain.

Let them soar—I'll take my space,
And meet myself at my own pace.
If I am late, I'll still arrive—
Bruised, but burning and still alive.

15. Three Skies, One Sun

They said it would feel like freedom here,
But I'm shackled by choices, tied to fear.
Caps flew high and dreams looked wide,
Now I flinch at questions I try to hide.

A job means peace, or so they say—
But peace feels hollow when dreams decay.
A paycheck's nice, it pays the dues,
But does it quiet the soul I'll lose?

Starting something of my own sounds brave,
But what if I fail? Who's left to save?
Will I still be enough without a win—
If my risks cost more than they bring in?

And then there's this thing I never named,
A passion too soft to be acclaimed.
It won't feed mouths or pay the rent,
But it's the only place my time feels well spent.

Everyone says, "Choose what you love,"
But what if I love more than one?
What if I'm cursed by stars above,
To chase three skies with just one sun?

Every scroll shows someone ahead,
Wedding rings, job offers, things I dread.
While I sit here stuck in my room,
Overthinking myself into gloom.

Friends are moving, building, flying—
And I keep clapping, while inside I'm dying.
Not out of envy, not out of spite—
Just tired of faking I'm alright.

My parents wait with patient grace,
Still see a child in my adult face.
And though they never say it loud,
I feel their worry, thick as a cloud.

I fear regret more than I fear lack,
Fear losing years I'll never get back.
Fear waking one day with success in hand,
But a heart too numb to understand.

What if none of this is wrong or right?
Just steps I take alone at night?

What if I try and still come undone?
What if that's how the brave are won?

34

So I'll carry this chaos, shoulder the weight,
Walk not with answers, but with faith.
The map is torn, the path's begun—
But I'll keep chasing *three skies, one sun.*

16. The Only Thing I Want Back

Out of all the things I've ever lost,
The love, the time, the weight I've tossed—
The friends who faded, the dreams that died,
The moments when I cried inside.

There's only one thing I long to find,
A piece of me, a state of mind.
Not the things that slipped through my hands,
But the person I used to be, the one I understand.

I lost myself in giving too much,
In trying to please, in a clutching touch.
I gave up pieces, little by little,
Chasing approval, lost in the middle.

I let the noise drown out my voice,
Silencing my heart, silencing choice.
I ran in circles, just to be seen,
Forgetting the beauty in what's unseen.

Out of all the things that drifted away,
The only loss I regret each day,
Is not the love or the plans I made—
But the me I buried, afraid to stay.

So I'll search for myself in the quiet places,
In the stillness, in the spaces,
Where I was lost but can now be found—
The person I was, but had to unbind.

Out of all the things I've ever lost,
The only one I want back is me, at all costs.
Not the past or the things that have been—
But the strength, the soul, the voice within.

17. The Process of Becoming

There's no rush in this journey, no need to race,
It's not about the finish line, but the steps we trace.
You'll stumble, you'll fall but that's part of the game,
Unlearning the old and learning what's new again.

It's okay if you feel lost, if you're unsure,
The path you're building now will make you more.
You've been broken, bent but you'll find your way,
Piece by piece, day by day.

You'll shed the skin that once felt tight,
Let go of the things that held you in fright.
You'll rebuild from dust, from loss, from pain,
And in the end, you'll find what you've gained.

This process of becoming—let it be slow,
Embrace the discomfort, let the old go.
You're not who you were yesterday,
And that's the beauty of today.

You'll unlearn the lies you told yourself,
And learn to place your worth on the shelf
That holds your truth, your heart, your soul,
Building yourself up, making yourself whole.

So don't rush, don't fear the time you take,
The pieces will fit, no need to fake.
Enjoy this moment, the growth, the change—
Because becoming yourself is never strange.

And one day you'll look back and see,
The person you've become, wild and free.
A masterpiece painted in every hue—
The joy of becoming, the joy of you.

18. Like the Moon, So Am I

Some days I shine, full-faced and bright,
A mirror to the world's delight.
I laugh too loud, I take up space—
I wear my joy without disgrace.

Then slowly, pieces start to wane,
A quiet ache I can't explain.
I fade from crowds, avoid the light,
And lose myself to silent night.

A half of me is left to show,
The rest is hidden deep below.
Still breathing, still I play my part,
But something's tugging at my heart.

The crescent phase, a sliver thin—
Is when I tuck my feelings in.
I'm softer then, unsure, not weak—
Just choosing peace instead of speak.

The gibbous girl, I almost gleam,
But feel I'm falling short of dream.
Not quite enough, not far from whole,
Still chasing pieces of my soul.

And when I'm new—completely gone,
I fear they'll think I can't go on.
But I am still here, still alive,
Still finding ways to bend and thrive.

Each phase of me, a truth I bear,
Not brokenness, but love laid bare.
I change, I shift, I dim, I glow—
But even then, I always grow.

You see me less, and think I hide,
But I'm just resting from the tide.
And though my light may not appear—
I'm just as whole, I'm always here.

19. Like the Sky

I want to be like the sky—vast and free,
Unapologetically, fiercely, fully me.
To own my thunders when I break apart,
And wear my storms like works of art.

Let my lightning speak when words fall short,
Let silence echo what I can't retort.
I won't stay quiet just to keep the peace,
My roar deserves its own release.

I want to cry out loud, not hide the rain,
To show the world my honest pain.
No shame in floods or cloudy days,
My softness holds a thousand ways.

I'll carry every shade, each hue and tone,
The darkness too—I'll make it known.
For even rage has room to breathe,
And every scar a truth beneath.

Like sunsets bleeding into dawn,
I'll wear my colors, bruised but strong.
Not just the light, but every shade—
Even the parts that feel afraid.

So let them stare, let them not understand,
My chaos is mine, it isn't planned.
I am the sky—too wild to bind,
A storm, a calm, a brilliant mind.

20. It's Scary Because It's New

Hey, I know it feels like a lot right now.
Everything's new and you're wondering how.
But trust me when I say, it's not that you can't,
It's just the unknown that makes your heart chant.

You've been through tougher days, you've stood tall,
This new thing? It's just a different kind of call.
I know it feels like you're standing on the edge,
But you've walked paths before, remember that pledge.

It's okay to be scared, I get that, I do,
But it's not because you're weak or untrue.
It's because this is different, this road's never been here,
And yeah, that's why it stirs up all this fear.

But let me remind you, just for a sec,
That fear's just a feeling—it's not a wreck.
It's part of the journey, part of the climb,
And it doesn't mean you won't do just fine.

I've seen you face storms and come out strong,
So why doubt yourself when you know you belong?
You've got everything you need inside,
The courage, the strength, the will to ride.

So take a *deep breath*, take it slow,
The first step is the hardest, that much I know.
But you can do this, just wait and see,
It's scary because it's new but that's not your decree.

You're not incapable, far from that,
You've got everything it takes, just like that.
So go ahead, take that leap,
And know you're capable of more than you think, *my
dear, just take the leap.*

21. When I Asked for Flowers

I asked God for flowers, gentle and bright,
A meadow of colors, a soft kind of light.
But he sent me clouds that wept with pain—
Not petals, not perfume—just endless rain.

I begged for ease, for paths lined in bloom,
He gave me storms and skies full of gloom.
I thought it cruel, thought he'd misheard,
My prayers dissolved without a word.

But slowly I learned what the rain could grow,
That even the thorns had seeds below.
Each drop carved strength where I felt lack,
And gave me roots I never knew I had.

The flowers I wanted? They came with time—

Not from sun alone, but the uphill climb.
I bloomed because I learned to bend,
To soak in grief and still transcend.

So now when I ask, I ask with grace—
Not just for gifts, but for the pace.
For now I know: though storms cause strain,
I asked for flowers...He gave me rain.